PAKISTAN: FRIEND OR FOE IN THE FIGHT AGAINST TERRORISM?

JOINT HEARING

BEFORE THE

SUBCOMMITTEE ON TERRORISM, NONPROLIFERATION, AND TRADE

AND THE

SUBCOMMITTEE ON ASIA AND THE PACIFIC

OF THE

COMMITTEE ON FOREIGN AFFAIRS
HOUSE OF REPRESENTATIVES

ONE HUNDRED FOURTEENTH CONGRESS

SECOND SESSION

JULY 12, 2016

Serial No. 114–173

Printed for the use of the Committee on Foreign Affairs

Available via the World Wide Web: http://www.foreignaffairs.house.gov/ or
http://www.gpo.gov/fdsys/

U.S. GOVERNMENT PUBLISHING OFFICE

20–742PDF WASHINGTON : 2016

For sale by the Superintendent of Documents, U.S. Government Publishing Office
Internet: bookstore.gpo.gov Phone: toll free (866) 512–1800; DC area (202) 512–1800
Fax: (202) 512–2104   Mail: Stop IDCC, Washington, DC 20402–0001

COMMITTEE ON FOREIGN AFFAIRS

EDWARD R. ROYCE, California, *Chairman*

CHRISTOPHER H. SMITH, New Jersey
ILEANA ROS-LEHTINEN, Florida
DANA ROHRABACHER, California
STEVE CHABOT, Ohio
JOE WILSON, South Carolina
MICHAEL T. McCAUL, Texas
TED POE, Texas
MATT SALMON, Arizona
DARRELL E. ISSA, California
TOM MARINO, Pennsylvania
JEFF DUNCAN, South Carolina
MO BROOKS, Alabama
PAUL COOK, California
RANDY K. WEBER SR., Texas
SCOTT PERRY, Pennsylvania
RON DeSANTIS, Florida
MARK MEADOWS, North Carolina
TED S. YOHO, Florida
CURT CLAWSON, Florida
SCOTT DesJARLAIS, Tennessee
REID J. RIBBLE, Wisconsin
DAVID A. TROTT, Michigan
LEE M. ZELDIN, New York
DANIEL DONOVAN, New York

ELIOT L. ENGEL, New York
BRAD SHERMAN, California
GREGORY W. MEEKS, New York
ALBIO SIRES, New Jersey
GERALD E. CONNOLLY, Virginia
THEODORE E. DEUTCH, Florida
BRIAN HIGGINS, New York
KAREN BASS, California
WILLIAM KEATING, Massachusetts
DAVID CICILLINE, Rhode Island
ALAN GRAYSON, Florida
AMI BERA, California
ALAN S. LOWENTHAL, California
GRACE MENG, New York
LOIS FRANKEL, Florida
TULSI GABBARD, Hawaii
JOAQUIN CASTRO, Texas
ROBIN L. KELLY, Illinois
BRENDAN F. BOYLE, Pennsylvania

AMY PORTER, *Chief of Staff* THOMAS SHEEHY, *Staff Director*
JASON STEINBAUM, *Democratic Staff Director*

(III)

CONTENTS

PAKISTAN: FRIEND OR FOE IN THE FIGHT AGAINST TERRORISM?

TUESDAY, JULY 12, 2016

House of Representatives,
Subcommittee on Terrorism, Nonproliferation, and Trade
and
Subcommittee on Asia and the Pacific,
Committee on Foreign Affairs,
Washington, DC.

The subcommittees met, pursuant to notice, at 2 o'clock p.m., in room 2172 Rayburn House Office Building, Hon. Matt Salmon (chairman of the Subcommittee on Asia and the Pacific) presiding.

Mr. Salmon. The subcommittee will come to order.

Good afternoon. I would like to thank my colleagues for joining me in convening this important joint subcommittee hearing. Unfortunately, Chairman Poe couldn't join us today, but I know he is very interested and engaged on the many challenges presented to the U.S. policymakers in Pakistan.

I would like to ask unanimous consent that his opening statement be inserted for the record. And, without objection, the hearing record will remain open for 5 business days to allow for further statements, questions, and extraneous materials for the record, subject to the length limitation in the rules.

As we all know, the United States has spent tens of billions in taxpayer dollars in the form of aid to Pakistan since 9/11, all in the hope that Pakistan would become a partner in the fight against terrorism. Unfortunately, despite this significant investment, Pakistani military and intelligence services are still linked to terrorist groups.

While the administration and the Pakistanis argue that there have been some successes in the fight against terrorist elements, particularly in Shawal Valley, terrorist organizations with close ties to Pakistan's military elite have been left untouched to the point of thriving while Pakistan's governing elite turns a blind eye.

Today we will discuss the administration's policy toward Pakistan and take a closer look at U.S. goals and expectations and options with Pakistan. The U.S.-Pakistan relationship has always been complicated. Pakistan is an important country of over 200 million people. It has nuclear capabilities and is strategically located with important neighbors, including China, India, and Afghanistan. But this country poses challenges that have plagued the United States for decades.

Given its significance, we can't afford to be spontaneous with our policy toward Pakistan as there could be far-reaching consequences. At the same time, many of us in Congress are unwilling to continue down this same failed path that consists of stacks of U.S. aid dollars without much support in the fight against terrorists to show for it. To be frank, Pakistan likes the United States because for decades we have given them a substantial amount of aid, especially to the Pakistani military, while they hope that they can prevent us from getting too close with India.

The United States tolerates Pakistan because it claims to be in the fight with us on the global war on terror. Recent history shows us that while Pakistan is getting money and weapons, U.S. goals in the war on terror are sadly lacking, and Pakistan may in fact be using the assets we provide them to undermine some of our strategic diplomatic efforts in the region.

Pakistan claims to be fighting terrorism, but they refuse to fight some groups who we know to be terrorists. Many observers see Pakistani forces as selective in the terrorist groups it fights, leaving others to continue to wreak havoc, especially when those groups target India.

Let us not forget that Pakistan was less than helpful in the hunt and ultimately demise of Osama bin Laden. And, to this day, they are holding Dr. Shakil Afridi under arrest, a hero to our country, for aiding in bin Laden's capture. Patience is growing very thin.

The recent failure to get consensus on the proposed F-16 sale is evidence of the newly endemic weariness where Pakistan is concerned. If our current efforts in Pakistan are not producing the results we seek, then what are our options? We could simply turn the money off, saving taxpayers billions of dollars. We could enforce sanctions or designate Pakistan as a State Sponsor of Terrorism. Sanctions were used in the '90s but without much effect.

I hope to hear from our witnesses as to what sort of stick and carrot approach might actually work with Pakistan, so we can have a strategic partnership on issues of mutual interest.

Fifteen years have passed since 9/11. Billions of dollars have been spent, and far too little change has occurred in Pakistan. Should we continue our failed policy and attempt to convince ourselves that Pakistan will one day see eye to eye with the United States, or should we look at the U.S.-Pakistan relationship through a new lens?

I look forward to today's constructive discussion to guide our policy efforts with Pakistan, and I turn to the ranking member, Mr. Sherman, for any comments that he might have.

Mr. SHERMAN. Thank you. We have relations with I think close to 200 countries. The default position is we don't give them money. So those who suggest aid to Pakistan have got to show that there is a strong justification for doing so. The evidence is not encouraging.

General Musharraf spoke on television in February about how Pakistan supported—provided support for Lashkar-e-Tayyiba, also known as LeT, and to the JeM, and essentially said terrorism was fine as long as it is directed at India. His remarks didn't provoke much of a reaction because much of the power structure in Pakistan agrees with him.

The Pakistani Government, as our chairman just pointed out, continues to hold Dr. Afridi. So not only do they shelter bin Laden, they punish those who helped us unshelter bin Laden. And the military establishment in Pakistan stokes paranoia about India, meddles in Afghanistan, and seems to be trying to weaken Afghanistan, so as to have a divided Pashtun population.

Regardless of how we answer the friend or foe question, our relationship with Pakistan is important. But keep in mind, you would think we would only provide aid to those countries where we don't have to ask the question: Friend or foe? But Pakistan is a nation of 180 billion people with a history of terrorist activities, 100 nuclear weapons, very confused body politic. The administration is requesting money for Pakistan in a number of different accounts, including 740 million of assistance on the civilian side, 265 million on the military side, and aid in other categories as well.

You would think that we would at least condition a large portion of this aid on the release of Dr. Afridi and his family. Providing more assistance to a government that has supported terrorists and has shown itself not very capable or serious about combatting terrorism may not be the very best use of taxpayer money.

We should be looking to reorient the money we do spend. I would like to focus on three things: Human rights, education, and public diplomacy. First, the Pakistani Government has a regrettable record of oppressing some of the major components of its country, large minorities, including the Sindh and the Baloch. Free speech and political dialogue are restricted.

Extrajudicial killings are common. For example, Anwar Leghari, the brother of a dear friend of mine, was assassinated in Sindh just last year, and the Pakistani Government has closed the file. I want to thank our State Department for at least raising a question. They have reopened the file, but that doesn't mean they will actually do anything.

A country with blasphemy laws is just begging individuals to claim that minorities have said this or that, unprovable, and them impose terrible penalties on someone they happen to dislike. It is no surprise that extremism flourishes in this environment.

Second, education. Pakistan must reform its education system. Many textbooks contain content that perpetuates minority stereotypes and feeds support for Islamic extremism. A lack of government-funded schools has led to an increase in the number of extremist madrassas in Sindh and other places in Pakistan. Girls are often denied education.

As I proposed I think at our last hearing, if we do provide aid, we ought to provide free textbooks, so that parents don't have that burden, aren't tempted to send their kids to a madrassa, and so that the textbooks, while they may not reflect all red, white, and blue values, will at least not contain material that would be an anathema to the American people.

And, finally, it is very hard for corrupt people to steal textbooks, especially in a country where the textbooks are made free by the American people.

I co-chair the Sindh Caucus, and so I focused on southern Pakistan in particular. And I have worked to make sure that we communicate to Sindh and other parts of Pakistan through Voice of

America in the language people speak in their homes. The importance of Pakistan seems to be so overwhelming that we spend billions of dollars giving it to a government that supports terrorism, but we don't spend $1.5 broadcasting in the Sindhi language. What a bizarre approach. What a pro-Islamabad approach. What an approach that does not match America's interest.

Finally, if we are going to win over the Muslim world, we need to have the State Department maybe hire one or a few people—fewer people that are experts in the 1800s European diplomacy and hire at least one person whose job description says ''understand the Quran, the hadith,'' you don't have to write a fatwa but you should have read 1,000 of them.

To think that we are waging a war for the minds of Muslims around the world and haven't hired a single person because of their understanding of that religion and how it is used and how it is misused shows an insular thinking in a bureaucracy that prizes an understanding of the machinations of metronic in European diplomacy two centuries ago.

I yield back.

Mr. SALMON. Thank you. In the interest of time—I know we have got other vote series coming up on the floor very soon—I will just yield one more slot before we go to the witnesses to the ranking member of the Subcommittee on Terrorism, Nonproliferation, and Trade, Mr. Keating.

Mr. KEATING. Thank you, Mr. Chairman. Thank you, Chairman Salmon, for conducting this hearing. I also would like to thank Mr. Rohrabacher and—who is here—I guess Mr. Poe as well, Ranking Member Sherman, and I would like to thank all the members that took the time to be here in this important hearing.

Of course, I would like to thank our panel for being here to discuss the topic at hand—Pakistan. Since 9/11, the United States' relationship with Pakistan has ebbed and flowed. Over the last decade and a half, several missteps have taken both sides into controversy, including instances of miscommunication, competing national interest, and fundamental failure to broaden and deepen the relationship as a whole.

Indeed, it seems that the two countries trend toward a one-dimensional transactional relationship centered along security concerns, instead of a broad partnership that includes trade and cultural linkages, is something that is problematic. However, over the last few years, even the security concerns have not equated to a smooth relationship. While Islamabad has helped the United States capture and kill numerous al-Qaeda members, including several senior leaders in its support for groups like Taliban, the Haqqani Network, Lashkar-e-Tayyiba, these things undermine critical U.S. national security interest.

Further complicating the issue is the fact that both leaders of the Taliban were killed or died within Pakistani borders, and the former head of al-Qaeda, Osama bin Laden, was also killed in Pakistan, only miles from the country's capital. There is little reason to suggest that Pakistan is going to change its strategic calculus.

It is critical that we vigorously consider our relationship with Pakistan and recognize that Islamabad is a willing and able partner in certain areas, while hostile in others. To be sure, accepting this paradigm does not mean abandoning Pakistan altogether. At stake in the region are some of America's most vital national security interests, including ensuring that neither Afghanistan nor Pakistan serves as a safe haven for global terrorists, keeping Pakistan's nuclear weapons out of the hands of terrorists and preventing war between India and Pakistan that could potentially go nuclear.

These interests warrant continued outreach and cooperation with Islamabad. To that end, the United States should consider a more balanced approach when supplying aid, an approach that favors education and economic aid over military assistance. The provision of U.S. weapons cannot reshape Pakistan's will to maintain its militant proxies on its western border, but those weapons do equip Pakistan to challenge India on its eastern border.

I look forward to hearing from our witnesses today and seeing how we can shape this relationship to the benefit of both countries.

With that, I yield back.

Mr. SALMON. Thank you. We are grateful to be joined today by Ambassador Zalmay Khalilzad. Appreciate you being here, Ambassador. And Mr. Bill Roggio, appreciate you being here. And Tricia Bacon.

And, Ambassador, we will yield the first time to you.

STATEMENT OF THE HONORABLE ZALMAY KHALILZAD, COUN-SELOR, CENTER FOR STRATEGIC AND INTERNATIONAL STUDIES

Ambassador KHALILZAD. Thank you very much, Chairman. I want to thank the ranking member, the chairman of the Terrorism Subcommittee, and all the distinguished members who are here. I appreciate the opportunity to appear and to make a few comments on a very important and difficult subject, the issue of Pakistan.

As you said, Chairman, it requires a deliberate but frank discussion and analysis of where we are and where we need to go. I have prepared a testimony, which I will submit for the record.

Mr. SALMON. Without objection, your formal testimony will be injected into the record.

Ambassador KHALILZAD. I would like to summarize that testimony by making a few points and look forward to the discussion.

While Pakistan, in the aftermath of 9/11, did provide significant help in the overthrow of the Taliban and in the capture of quite a number of al-Qaeda members, I think it fair to say that if one focuses on Afghanistan, which would be the burden of my comments today, looking at Pakistan, one can conclude now the following.

First, Pakistan is now a State Sponsor of Terror. There is no question that the Pakistani military and the Pakistani intelligence agency, the ISI, the Inter-Service Agency, supports the Haqqani Network, which we regard—the United States has regarded as a terrorist organization. One of our former chairmen of the Joint Chiefs called the Haqqani Network a virtual arm of the ISI.

Point two, it is also clear that the Pakistani military and Pakistani intelligence provide sanctuary and support for the Taliban, which is an extremist organization that provided sanctuary for al-Qaeda in the early period, and even recently the leader of al-

Qaeda, Zawahiri, pledged allegiance to the new leader of the Taliban. So the relationship continues.

And these two steps that Pakistan clearly has taken—it used to deny that there were any Taliban in Pakistan. When I was Ambassador to Afghanistan, when I went to see President Musharraf, and after a long discussion when I raised the issue of the Taliban with him, he asked me, ''They are not here. Give me their phone number. Give me their address.'' I had to remind him that the leadership of the Taliban was called the Quetta Shura, which, you know, is a big Pakistani city, and there is also—there was Peshawar Shura, which is another big city in Pakistan, and the media regularly went and interviewed some of these people.

But, in any case, as you know, more recently he has boasted, Mr. Musharraf, that he did obviously help the Taliban and the Haqqani Network. But the Pakistani support for these two groups has been a critical factor in my judgment in the longevity and successes that these two groups have had against the United States, against our forces.

We have lost quite a lot of people, as you know, military in particular, but also non-military folks, and they have imposed huge financial costs by making the war prolonged and significant, requiring us to invest not only life but also resources, and it has imposed huge costs also, both military and civilian, on the Afghans.

Those of us who have studied insurgencies and counterinsurgencies, if there is a sanctuary, it makes it much harder, it takes longer, becomes more protracted to defeat that insurgency. I am not saying other factors are not important; they are. I mean, the question of governance, policies of the government in charge, but sanctuaries make it much harder to defeat insurgencies.

So it seems to me that our policy, if I would characterize it, as one of engagement, providing support, sometimes withholding some assistance, but one of assistance, has not produced what we had hoped would be the result in Pakistan, which is that they would change policy to bring the Taliban to the negotiating table and move against those Taliban that are not reconcilable or would not reconcile and then also to move against the Haqqani Network. This has not happened.

So, as a nation, in my view, it is important that we debate what to do next. And I believe that we need to consider a different policy among our options, and the policy that I think is worthy of consideration is one of increasing the cost of this policy to Pakistan.

You know, typically, when you want to discourage bad behavior, you have to do things that look like punishment or imposing costs to shape a response. And Pakistan has believed so far correctly that they can get aid, billions, and get support and continue to do these things, and that we would not confront them with the choice of either you take our assistance or—and you can stop what you are doing or there will be no assistance.

And I think unless we effect fundamentally that calculus, that they confront the choice, it is unlikely that they would adjust the policy that we require, that the Afghans require, and indeed the world requires. I welcome some of the recent announcement by the administration and some of the actions, such as the drone attack against Mullah Mansour in Pakistan, I think that sent a strong message.

I believe that the administration's effort to isolate Pakistan, to pressure it more, is welcome, but I think it is insufficient. We need to do more. And more, in my judgment, is, one, we need to do additional drone attacks against targets that are Haqqani and Taliban related.

If Pakistan does not move against the Haqqani Network and the irreconcilable Taliban, we need to have, in my judgment, very sharply focused sanctions against people in these two institutions, the military, especially the Army, and the intelligence network, were involved in support of the Haqqani Network and the Taliban, and that would mean financial sanctions and, in my view, also it means travel to the United States.

I think we ought to suspend all non-humanitarian and non-education assistance to Pakistan. I agree with the ranking member that education is very important, and we ought to continue with educational assistance, humanitarian assistance, but non-education, not only our own, but in IMF I think we need to use our influence there to make sure that the next package that is likely to come up later this summer or early fall does not go through without Pakistan taking the necessary measures with regard to these two groups.

I also think we ought to consider, deliberate, debate whether Pakistan should not be put on the list, State Department list of sponsors of terrorism. Factually, it is. Now, the question is, what are the pros and cons? And I think there are costs for us not doing this, because the whole less than problem becomes—loses its legitimacy when a state clearly is doing something and we are not calling a spade a spade, and that has its own cost.

And I also believe that calling Pakistan a major non-NATO ally, given what it is doing, also raises questions of the legitimacy of such a designation. We ought to signal that without a change on these two issues we would recalibrate, reconsider that designation.

And I would think that we ought to also, as we do with regard to North Korea, a country that has nuclear weapons but has many hostile and negative domestic and external policies, consider as to when we might take the whole issue to the Security Council, in collaboration with the Afghans, to expose—we have not done as much as we could, in my view, to expose the details of how this policy of support for Haqqani and for the Taliban are actually conducted by Pakistan and the implications, the ramifications of that in terms of the amount of damage it has done to fellow Muslims in Afghanistan, besides the killings that have taken place of the coalition forces who are there.

I think also, as we think down the road, given that Pakistan may choose not to respond favorably to this, we need to look at the strengthening cooperation with India on terrorism and counterterrorism and on strengthening Afghanistan, that it can be hardened as—my judgment is that if we do the steps that I have described, it is not out of the question that Pakistan might reconsider, because I think if we can shake this belief that they have that they can continue to be both the beneficiary of U.S. assistance and continue to do what they are doing with regard to the Taliban and the

8

Haqqani Network, with the view that eventually we will tire out—
we will get tired, we will leave, and then they can go back to imposing a Taliban government on Afghanistan, and the good days
will be here again from their perspective regionally, we will have
to look at other ways with others who share our perspective on terrorism, particularly India. And I just was there last week, very serious discussions, I think we will need to take a look at this.

I understand, Mr. Chairman, as a final point, that this is not an
easy issue. The administration that I was a part of, we tried engagement, too, and assistance in the golden hour after 9/11 when
our credibility was high, we didn't push as hard Pakistan at that
time, as we should have.

I think another golden hour may have become available after the
killing of Mullah Mansour, but by itself I think it is insufficient.
We need to get Pakistan's attention, and that things are different,
that they do need to make a choice, and I recommended the steps
that I did for your consideration.

Thank you, Chairman.

[The prepared statement of Ambassador Khalilzad follows:]

ZALMAY KHALILZAD

FORMER U.S. AMBASSADOR TO IRAQ, AFGHANISTAN AND U.N.;
COUNSELOR, CENTER FOR STRATEGIC AND INTERNATIONAL STUDIES

HOUSE COMMITTEE ON FOREIGN AFFAIRS: SUBCOMMITTEE ON TERRORISM,
NONPROLIFERATION, AND TRADE

JULY 12, 2016

PAKISTAN: FRIEND OR FOE IN THE FIGHT AGAINST TERRORISM?

Mr. Chairman and members of the Committee:

Thank you for the opportunity to offer my assessment and advice on the issue of Pakistan's support for terrorist and extremist forces. Pakistani proxies pose a severe threat to coalition and Afghan forces and civilians.

Indeed, Pakistani policy is the principal cause of the ongoing conflict in Afghanistan.

More broadly, Pakistan's use of extremist and terrorist proxies – including to threaten India -- is a significant contributor to the global menace of Islamic extremism. It must be confronted if we are to succeed in defeating terrorism and extremism around the world.

Background

Since the overthrow of the Taliban regime after 9/11, Pakistan has been playing a perfidious and dangerous double game. It has portrayed itself as a U.S. partner, yet supports the Taliban and the al-Qaeda-linked Haqqani network.

Since 2005, the Taliban and Haqqani network have regrouped in Pakistan and waged a devastating insurgency against U.S. and Afghan forces.

Poor governance by the Afghan government is a factor in Kabul's inability to defeat the insurgents. But the Taliban's resilience can be attributed above all to the strategic decision of the Pakistani military and intelligence services to provide sanctuary and support to these groups.

Pakistan's Goals

Pakistan views the Taliban as an effective proxy to ensure Pakistani dominance over Afghanistan.

Islamabad also believes that continuing the war in Afghanistan will lead to a U.S. withdrawal, which would change the balance of power against the current government and in favor of its proxies.

Ultimately, Pakistan seeks the overthrow of the current government in Afghanistan because it is not compliant.

Declaratory Policy vs. Actual Policy

Pakistan understands that its double-game is risky, but it believes that the risk is manageable. Pakistani leaders reason that they can continue to receive U.S. assistance and avoid international isolation even if they support the Taliban and Haqqani network. They have seen little evidence that Washington will force it to choose between U.S. support and its alliance with the Taliban.

Every country has a gap between its declaratory policy and its actual policy. In the case of Pakistan, the gap is huge. Until recently, Pakistani leaders even denied that there were Taliban in their country!

Pakistan believes that they can outmaneuver and outwait us. They are adept at offering tactical gestures that make it appear they are being helpful, which they calculate will make it more difficult for the U.S. to take a hardline stance.

I have first-hand experience in this regard. As I document in my recently published memoir—*The Envoy*-- the President asked me in 2005 to visit Pakistani dictator General Pervez Musharraf and raise the issue of the Taliban sanctuaries. When I asked Gen. Musharraf why Pakistan was sponsoring the Taliban, he denied that there were any Taliban in Pakistan. He refused to acknowledge that the leadership of the Taliban were residing in Quetta or contend with the fact that its ruling Council bore the name of the capital of Baluchistan. Musharraf instead insisted that I provide him with the names and phone numbers of the Taliban in Afghanistan. Years later, when he was no longer his country's leader, he boasted to the world of his country's support for the extremist group.

Recommendations

The May 21 killing of Taliban leader Mullah Akhtar Mansour in a U.S. drone strike has created a golden hour to confront Pakistan. Washington can force Islamabad to make a choice: U.S. aid and international support or a continued relationship with the Haqqani network and irreconcilable Taliban.

Catalyzing a decisive effect on Pakistani policy, however, will require the U.S. to escalate pressure on Islamabad. Otherwise the opportunity will dissipate.

For Islamabad to break with the Haqqani network and the Taliban, the Pakistani leadership needs to see that continued support for the insurgency will come at a high price.

Escalating drone strikes against Haqqani and irreconcilable Taliban leaders would deliver that message, but drone strikes alone will not be enough without corresponding political and financial pressure.

On the financial side, Pakistan has been an enormous beneficiary of international support -- specifically from Coalition support funds, bilateral assistance, and multilateral assistance from the IMF and World Bank. In addition to cutting off this assistance, Washington should warn Pakistan that it will face escalating financial sanctions—like those once imposed on Iran—unless it facilitates reconciliation talks between the Afghan government and the Taliban.

As an initial step, the U.S. can impose financial and travel restrictions on senior Pakistani officials known to be complicit in the insurgency, and freeze funds in U.S. banks belonging to Pakistani entities—both military and corporate—involved in financing the Taliban.

Politically, Pakistan cannot be a member in good standing of the international community so long as its agencies or military services aggress against Afghanistan.

Pakistan is currently designated by the United States as a "major non-NATO ally." This status is wholly inappropriate. Pakistan's current policy and conduct would better merit its inclusion on the State Department's list of state-sponsors of terrorism.

The U.N. Security Council is an appropriate venue in which to raise Pakistan's aggression against Afghanistan. To help secure international support for a U.S.-Afghan-sponsored resolution condemning Pakistan, the U.S. should declassify and broadcast information indicating Pakistani support for the insurgency and its narcotics trafficking.

Action at the Security Council would also provide the United States to ask China, one of Pakistan's staunchest allies, whether it wants to be saddled with another North Korea – a rogue, isolated state surviving on Beijing's dole.

I thank you, Mr. Chairman, for your consideration on this issue. I look forward to your questions.

———

Mr. SALMON. Thank you very much, Ambassador.

On the clocks, please look at the amber light and the red lights. I am not going to hold you to—this is too important an issue, and we want to hear everything that you have to say, but I know we have a lot of questions up here, too.

Mr. Roggio.

STATEMENT OF MR. BILL ROGGIO, SENIOR EDITOR, LONG WAR JOURNAL, FOUNDATION FOR DEFENSE OF DEMOCRACIES

Mr. ROGGIO. Thank you, sir. Chairman Salmon, Ranking Members Sherman and Keating, and the rest of the committees, thank you very much for having us here today to talk about this extremely important issue.

You properly asked the question of whether Pakistan is a friend or a foe, and unequivocally the answer is a foe. Pakistan may combat some groups that threaten it—movement of the Taliban in Pakistan, Islamic movement in Uzbekistan, groups like that that are fighting the Pakistani State. However, they support numerous terrorist organizations, organizations that are listed by the U.S. Government as foreign terrorist organizations.

In my testimony, I list six and give a brief description of the activities, but we can list dozens or scores of groups that Pakistan supports in India, in Afghanistan, groups that are designated terrorist organizations, groups that provide aid and support for al-Qaeda, groups whose leaders serve as the deep bench for al-Qaeda and other terrorist groups when their leadership is winnowed down via drone strikes by the U.S. and Pakistan's tribal areas.

Again, the evidence is indisputable. Just this weekend, the Indians killed a Kashmiri terrorist who is a member of Hizb-ul-Mujahideen. This is a nasty terrorist organization. And, Pakistan, did they welcome this killing? No. In fact, they denounced it and referred to him as a Kashmiri separatist. This is an individual who recruits online for holy war and is recruiting youth and poisoning the youth to conduct terrorist attacks.

And lest we pretend that, well, this has just been in Pakistan an issue with Pakistan and Kashmir, it is not. These Kashmiri terrorist groups that have been aided by the Pakistani State base themselves in Afghanistan. I could list groups—Lashkar-e-Tayyiba, Harakat-ul-Mujahideen, who the State Department said as recently as 2014 is running training camps inside Afghanistan.

These groups are attacking and killing U.S. soldiers, and I haven't even touched on groups like the Taliban, the Haqqani Network, or the Mullah Nazir Group. These are just small groups. I concur—and for the interest of brevity and time—Ambassador Khalilzad's statements on the Afghan Taliban, Haqqani Network, I concur with 100 percent.

What the Pakistanis are doing, they are playing a fantastic shell game. They have this narrative called good Taliban versus bad Taliban. The good Taliban is any group that the Pakistani likes, and those are groups that don't attack the Pakistani State. These are groups that carry out Pakistan's foreign policy—Haqqani Network, Afghan Taliban, Mullah Nazir Group.

And then, even the Pakistan press referred to this, groups like Lashkar-e-Tayyiba, Hizb-ul-Mujahideen, Harakat-ul-Mujahideen—again, I could go down the list. They are considered ''good Taliban'' as well. And the bad Taliban, they are the ones that fight the Pakistani State. They are the ones being targeted in the Shawal Valley, in North Waziristan. When the Pakistanis go after these groups, they pretend that they are going after the Haqqani Network or the Mullah Nazir Group or the Afghan Taliban, but they are not.

The Pakistanis haven't named a single high, mid-level, or low-level leader killed in one of these operations, because they haven't killed any of them. They haven't captured any of them, although they are selectively targeting in the interest of the Pakistani State.

As a matter of fact, this narrative of the good Taliban versus bad Taliban, my Web site, Long War Journal, has been banned in Pakistan for 4 years because we have reported on this narrative, and it has been an issue that I have not let go of, and we are banned because Pakistan has a history of killing individuals that expose these types of situations.

Syed Shahzad was brutally executed by the ISI for his reporting on links between Pakistan's Intelligence Service and al-Qaeda, and attacks that were occurring within Pakistan. You know, Pakistan is not going to change its calculus. These groups that they support, they are doing this because they feel it is their best chance in countering India, and that is why they support them.

I also believe there is an ideological aspect within large elements within the military and intelligence services as well, and this is being reported on. So you have this confluence of it helps their policy in India, as well as they get the ideological, you know, radical jihadist support as well.

These groups are strategic depth for Afghanistan in case it has to go to war, and it uses them in Afghanistan—I am sorry, strategic depth within Pakistan against India, and it uses these groups also to conduct its policy inside of Afghanistan to target and kill U.S. forces and allied forces.

We have to change our calculus if Pakistan won't change theirs, and I concur with Ambassador Khalilzad's statements we need to—I believe all funding should stop. We should put a brake on the situation until we can really get a handle on it. Money is fungible. If we are funding Pakistani education, they can fund Pakistani militants with the money they are saving.

We have to consider sanctions. We have to consider the possibility of state sponsorship of terrorism. Do we limit or cut off trade with Pakistan? Do we restrict Pakistani's travel to the United States, cut off visas, student visas? All of these options should be on the table, unless Pakistan changes its habits and its—we have been enabling the Pakistani State for 15 years now, nothing has changed, and it has only gotten worse.

Thank you very much.

[The prepared statement of Mr. Roggio follows:]

Congressional Testimony

Pakistan: Friend or Foe in the Fight against Terrorism?

Bill Roggio
Senior Editor
Long War Journal
Foundation for Defense of Democracies

Hearing before House Foreign Affairs Committee
Subcommittee on Terrorism, Nonproliferation, and Trade
Subcommittee on Asia and the Pacific

Washington, DC
July 12, 2016

FDD
FOUNDATION FOR
DEFENSE OF DEMOCRACIES

Bill Roggio   July 12, 2016

Chairman Poe and Chairman Salmon, Ranking Members Keating and Sherman, and other members of the Committees, thank you for inviting me here today to speak about Pakistan and its support for terrorist groups that threaten the security of the United States and its allies.

This Committee rightly asks the question of whether Pakistan is a friend or foe in the fight against terrorism. While Pakistani officials and forces have assisted the U.S. in hunting senior al Qaeda figures at times, Pakistan's overall strategy is pro-jihadist and therefore puts it in the foe category. Pakistan does battle some terrorist groups within its borders, but it only does so because these groups pose a direct threat to the state.

Pakistan myopically supports a host of terrorist groups in Pakistan, Afghanistan, and India to further its goals in the region. Pakistan backs these groups despite the fact that they are allied with and aid the very terrorist groups that fight the Pakistani state. In addition, many of the jihadist groups sponsored by Pakistan are allied with al Qaeda.

Today I will highlight six major groups directly supported or tolerated by Pakistan's establishment: the Afghan Taliban and its subgroup, the Haqqani Network; the Mullah Nazir Group, Lashkar-e-Taiba, Harakat-ul-Mujahideen, and Jaish-e-Mohammed. Each of these groups is used by Pakistan as an instrument of its foreign policy. These six groups are by no means the only terrorist organizations supported by Pakistan, they are merely the most prominent.

Pakistan uses these six groups and others as a counterweight against what its policy makers perceive to be Pakistan's greatest threat: India. However, the jihadist ideology has also spread throughout Pakistan as a result of policies adopted by the country's military elite. Therefore, we should not underestimate the degree to which these groups are supported for ideological reasons.[1]

Pakistan, a country of 182 million people, does not possess the manpower to counter India, a nation of 1.25 billion. Pakistan and India have been in a virtual state of war since Partition in 1947. The two countries have fought four active wars in 1947, 1965, 1971, and 1999. Each of these wars was initiated by Pakistan, and

---

[1] Ghafour, Hamida. (2013, August 26). Zia ul-Haq's legacy in Pakistan 'enduring and toxic'. thestar.com. Retrieved from
https://www.thestar.com/news/world/2013/08/26/zia_ulhaqs_legacy_in_pakistan_enduring_and_toxic.html

ended in defeats. Pakistani strategists have determined that to counter India, it must use unconventional means, including supporting jihadist groups.

Strategic Depth

To compensate for its inability to achieve victory on conventional battlefields against India, Pakistan implemented its own version of "strategic depth" in Afghanistan.[2] Pakistan has supported groups in Afghanistan in order to deny India influence in its backyard, as well as to allow the nation to serve as a fallback in case of an Indian invasion.

Pakistan capitalized on the chaos in Afghanistan post-Soviet withdrawal and hunted for a group that would serve its purposes. With the rise of Mullah Omar's Taliban faction in the early 1990s, Pakistan military and intelligence officers assigned to implement strategic depth saw the perfect partner: a powerful jihadist political movement that was gaining popularity throughout the country and was capable of sustaining military advances. Pakistan provided military and financial support to Omar's faction, which successfully established the Islamic Emirate of the Taliban in 1996 and controlled upwards of 90 percent of the country until the US invasion in 2001.

In addition to securing a friendly government in Afghanistan, Pakistan used the country as both a training and a recruiting ground for a host of jihadist groups that fight in India-occupied Kashmir.

Good vs Bad Taliban

In order to justify its policy of support to jihadist groups, Pakistani elites have attempted to distinguish between what are referred to as "good Taliban" and "bad Taliban." Simply stated, the so-called "good Taliban" are groups that advance Pakistan's foreign policy goals and do not threaten the state or wage war within its borders. "Good Taliban" and other groups deemed acceptable by the Pakistani establishment include the Afghan Taliban, the Haqqani Network, the Mullah Nazir Group, Lashkar-e-Taiba, Harakat-ul-Mujahideen, and Jaish-e-Mohammed. These groups conduct numerous heinous acts of terrorism in the region, and are directly

---

[2] Dalrymple, William. (2013, June 25). A Deadly Triangle. *The Brookings Essay*. Retrieved from http://www.brookings.edu/research/essays/2013/deadly-triangle-afghanistan-pakistan-india-c

responsible for the deaths of thousands of American soldiers and civilians, and yet are supported by the Pakistani state.

"Bad Taliban" are any jihadist faction that challenges the primacy of the Pakistani state. These groups include the Movement of the Taliban in Pakistan, the Turkistan Islamic Party, and the weakened Islamic Movement of Uzbekistan. The Pakistani military has pursued these groups in the Federally Administered Tribal Areas (FATA) and Khyber Pakhtunkhwa province with some success. However, when targeting these groups, the military has avoided pursuing groups such as the Haqqani Network, which provided shelter and support for the "bad Taliban."

Pakistani officials have denied that it pursues a policy of strategic depth and differentiates between "good and bad Taliban", or alternatively, have claimed it will no longer differentiate between the two.[3] However, these claims are false. This is demonstrated in Pakistan's continuing support for the aforementioned groups and others, as well as an unwillingness to round up leaders and key operatives of these groups.

The Afghan Taliban

Pakistan's support for the Afghan Taliban is well documented. It helped establish the group in the 1990s and continues to support it to this day. Hamid Gul, the former head of the Inter-Services Intelligence Directorate (ISI), Pakistan's military intelligence agency that developed and implemented the policy of strategic depth, is known as "the father of the Taliban" for his role in directing support to the Taliban. (Gul is also known as the "Godfather of terrorism" for his support of global jihadist groups.[4]) The term "father of the Taliban" isn't reserved only for Gul; Maulana Sami ul Haq, the director of the radical Darul Uloom Haqqania madrassa, also hold this title.[5] His madrassa feeds thousands of new recruits to the Taliban on a regular basis.

[3] Shahid, Kunwar Khulsune. (2015, January 19). Pakistan: No more 'Good Taliban'. *The Diplomat*. Retrieved from http://thediplomat.com/2015/01/pakistan-no-more-good-taliban/

[4] Riedel, Bruce. (2015, August 20). Terrors godfather. *Bookings*. Retrieved from http://www.brookings.edu/research/opinions/2015/08/20-terrors-godfather-hamid-gul-riedel

[5] Ali, Imtiaz. (2007, May 23). The Father of the Taliban: An interview with Maulana Sami-ul-Haq. *The Jamestown Foundation*. Retrieved from http://www.jamestown.org/programs/tm/single/?tx_ttnews%5Btt_news%5D=4180&tx_ttnews%5BbackPid%5D=26&cHash=2feb32fe98a6250c9fa2ab6610564cec#.V36AaJMrJZg

Bill Roggio   July 12, 2016

Afghanistan's insurgency continues to be fueled by Pakistan's military and intelligence services to this day. The Taliban's Quetta Shura, or supreme decision making council, has been based in the Pakistani city of the same name as well as elsewhere. The Taliban's four regional military commands all are named after Pakistani cities (Quetta, Peshawar, Miramshah, Gerdi Jangal).[6]

The Taliban's top leadership has been based inside Pakistan, with the knowledge and approval of the military and ISI. The Taliban's first two emirs died while in Pakistan. Mullah Omar, the Taliban's founder and first emir, died in a Pakistani hospital near Quetta in April 2013. His successor, Mullah Mansour, was killed by the US in a drone strike in Baluchistan two months ago. They and other senior, middle and lower level leaders have operated inside Pakistan without consequence.

Pakistan's border areas with Afghanistan serve as the life blood of the Taliban.

While all of Pakistan is jihadist friendly, the provinces of Khyber Pakhtunkhwa and Baluchistan are flush with Taliban recruiting centers, training camps, safe houses, and financial hubs. Taliban commanders freely admit that the ISI arms them and provides safe haven and training camps inside Pakistan.[7]

Meanwhile, radical madrassas throughout the country indoctrinate Pakistani youth into the jihadist worldview and send them off to fight for the Taliban and other allied groups.

The Haqqani Network

The Haqqani Network (HQN) is listed by the US as a Foreign Terrorist Organization for its support of al Qaeda and other terrorist groups. It is an integral part of the Taliban. Its founder, Jalaluddin Haqqani, is a member of the Quetta Shura, while his son is one of the two deputy emirs to Mullah Haibatullah, the new leader of the Taliban. Thirteen senior HQN are listed by the US as specially designated global terrorists; most, including Sirajuddin, have been directly linked to al Qaeda. Several top al Qaeda leaders were killed in US counterterrorism operations while being sheltered by HQN.

---

[6] Roggio, Bill. (2010, February 23). The Afghan Taliban's top leaders. *The Long War Journal*. Retrieved from http://www.longwarjournal.org/archives/2010/02/the_talibans_top_lea.php

[7] Agencies. (2011, October 27). ISI arming and training us, claim 'Taliban commanders'. *The Express Tribune*. Retrieved from http://tribune.com.pk/story/283051/isi-arming-and-training-us-claim-taliban-commanders/

Bill Roggio   July 12, 2016

Deadly HQN attacks inside Afghanistan have been directly traced back to
Pakistan. In one instance in 2011, HQN handlers, including Badruddin Haqqani,
directed an assault on a hotel in Kabul from Pakistan, according to Afghanistan's
National Directorate of Security.[8] A similar attack took place in Jalalabad that
same year.

In Pakistan, the HQN is based in North Waziristan and has a presence in other
Pakistani tribal agencies, such as Kurram, The Haqqanis run the notorious Manba
Ulom madrassa in Miramshah, North Waziristan.

Despite the HQN's overt links to al Qaeda, the group remains a darling of
Pakistan's military and ISI. When the Pakistani military conducts operations in the
FATA, it deliberately avoids the HQN. While Pakistani leaders insist the Haqqanis
are not excluded from operations, not a single senior, mid-level, or junior leader
has been killed or captured during Pakistani operations in the FATA from 2008 to
date.

The Mullah Nazir Group

The Mullah Nazir Group is a Pakistani Taliban faction that operates in South
Waziristan. The US government listed it as a specially designated global terrorist
entity in 2013 and said it "has run training camps, dispatched suicide bombers,
provided safe haven for al Qaeda fighters, and conducted cross-border operations
in Afghanistan against the United States and its allies."[9] Its current leader, Bahawal
Khan,[10] and his deputy, sub-commander Malang,[11] are also listed by the US as
specially designated global terrorists.

Its former leader, Mullah Nazir, who was killed in a US drone strike, identified
himself as a leader of al Qaeda and said he shared the group's views on global

---

[8] Joscelyn, Thomas and Roggio, Bill. (2011, September 3). Haqqani Network directed Kabul
    hotel assault by phone from Pakistan. *The Long War Journal*. Retrieved from
    http://www.longwarjournal.org/archives/2011/09/haqqani_network_dire.php

[9] US Department of State. (2013, February 26). Terrorist Designations of the Commander Nazir
    Group and Malang Wazir. Retrieved from
    http://www.state.gov/r/pa/prs/ps/2013/02/205195.htm

[10] US Department of State. (2013, August 6). Terrorist Designation of Bahawal Khan.
    Retrieved from http://www.state.gov/r/pa/prs/ps/2013/08/212730.htm

[11] US Department of State. (2013, February 26). Terrorist Designations of the Commander
    Nazir Group and Malang Wazir. Retrieved from
    http://www.state.gov/r/pa/prs/ps/2013/02/205195.htm

Bill Roggio   July 12, 2016

jihad.[12] Multiple al Qaeda leaders have been killed while sheltering with the Mullah Nazir Group.[13] The Pakistani military provided the Mullah Nazir Group with direct support when it clashed with rival members of the Islamic Movement of Uzbekistan.[14]

Despite the Mullah Nazir Group's direct ties to al Qaeda, Pakistan has viewed it as an ally in the tribal areas. Like the Haqqani Network, the Mullah Nazir Group was left untouched when the Pakistani military launched operations that targeted the Movement of the Taliban in Pakistan.

Lashkar-e-Taiba

Lashkar-e-Taiba (LeT) is perhaps the most blatant example of Pakistan's support for jihadists groups. Listed by the US as a Foreign Terrorist Organization, it was founded by its leader, Hafiz Saeed, along with Osama bin Laden and Abdullah Azzam, the godfather of international jihad. Bin Laden helped LeT establish training camps in Afghanistan's provinces of Kunar and Paktia,[15] where it continues to operates to this day. LeT shares al Qaeda's goal of establishing an Islamic state in South Asia and beyond.

LeT operates openly inside Pakistan and has offices throughout the country. Markaz-e-Taiba, its headquarters in Muridke near Lahore, is a sprawling complex that is used to indoctrinate future jihadists before they are sent off for military training. The provincial government of Punjab has financed Markaz-e-Taiba in the past.[16]

---

[12] Shahzad, Syed Saleem. (2011, May 5). Taliban and al-Qaeda: Friends in arms. *Asia Times*. Retrieved from http://www.atimes.com/atimes/South_Asia/ME05Df02.html

[13] Roggio, Bill. (2011, May 4). 'Good' Pakistani Taliban leader Nazir affirms membership in al Qaeda. *The Long War Journal*. Retrieved from http://www.longwarjournal.org/archives/2011/05/good_pakistani_taliban_leader_nazir_admits_membership_in_al_qaeda.php

[14] Abbas, Hassan. (2007, May 14). South Waziristan's Maulvi Nazir: The New Face of the Taliban. *The Jamestown Foundation*. Retrieved from http://www.jamestown.org/single/?no_cache=1&tx_ttnews%5Btt_news%5D=4147#.V36bd5MrJBw

[15] Tellis, Ashley J. (2010, March 11). Bad Company – Lashkar-e-Tayyiba and the growing ambition of Islamist militancy in Pakistan. *Carnegie Endowment*. Retrieved from http://carnegieendowment.org/files/0311_testimony_tellis.pdf

[16] Roul, Animesh. (2013 June 27). Punjab Government Financing Front Group for Lashkar-e-taiba Terrorists. *The Jamestown Foundation*. Retrieved from http://www.jamestown.org/single/?tx_ttnews%5Btt_news%5D=41078&no_cache=1#.V360HpMrJBw

Bill Roggio   July 12, 2016

This terrorist infrastructure was used to conduct egregious terrorist attacks in India and Afghanistan. The most prominent attack took place in Mumbai, India, when a suicide assault team fanned out across the city and targeted multiple locations, including a theater, a train station, hotels and a Jewish center and killed 164 people. The attack lasted for three days. Indian intelligence traced phone calls back to handlers in Pakistan as the assault was ongoing. The handlers directed its fighters to execute non-Muslims, often brutally, and laughed when their instructions were carried out. After the attack, Interpol issued arrest warrants for two serving senior Pakistani army officers and a retired major.[17]

Despite LeT's overt ties to al Qaeda and its campaign of terror in India and Afghanistan, the Pakistani government refuses to crack down on this group. Its complexes in Muridke and throughout the country remain open, and its leaders operate unfettered. Hafiz Saeed is feted by Pakistani officials, who refuse to hold him and other LeT leaders accountable for their actions. Not a single member of LeT who has been implicated in the Mumbai attack has been prosecuted.

Harakat-ul-Mujahideen

Harakat-ul-Mujahideen is yet another Pakistan-based jihadist group that has been listed by the US as a Foreign Terrorist Organization. Its emir, Fazle-ur-Rahman Khalil, is also named by the US as a specially designated global terrorist.[18]

In an update to the US designation of HuM in 2014, the US noted that it "operates in Pakistan, and engages in terrorist activity in Kashmir, India, Pakistan, and Afghanistan" and "also operates terrorist training camps in eastern Afghanistan."[19] These camps are thought to be in existence to this day.

---

[17] Nelson, Dean and Swami, Praveen. (2010, October 8). Interpol issues Pakistan army arrest warrants over Mumbai attacks. *The Telegraph.* Retrieved from http://www.telegraph.co.uk/news/worldnews/asia/pakistan/8050866/Interpol-issues-Pakistan-army-arrest-warrants-over-Mumbai-attacks.html

[18] Treasury Department Targets Senior Official and Support Networks of Two Pakistan-based Terrorist Groups. (2014, September 30). *U.S. Department of Treasury.* Retrieved from https://www.treasury.gov/press-center/press-releases/Pages/jl2653.aspx

[19] Roggio, Bill. (2014, August 8). Harkat-ul-Mujahideen 'operates terrorist training camps in eastern Afghanistan'. *The Long War Journal.* Retrieved from http://www.longwarjournal.org/archives/2014/08/harakat-ul-mujahidee.php

Khalil, like LeT's Saeed, is a made man inside Pakistan. In 2011, it was reported that he lived openly near the capital of Islamabad.[20] Khalil is one of the jihadists Osama bin Laden consulted before issuing his infamous fatwa declaring war against the US in 1998. Khalil also signed the fatwa. Osama bin Laden's courier was reportedly tied to HuM, which may have played a role in the al Qaeda master's support network inside Pakistan.[21] HuM has also acted like a feeder organization for al Qaeda's newest regional branch, Al Qaeda in the Indian Subcontinent (AQIS), which was officially established in September 2014. Asim Umar, the emir of AQIS, is a former member of HuM.[22]

Khalil has "dispatched fighters to India, Afghanistan, Somalia, Chechnya and Bosnia, was a confidante of bin Laden and hung out with 9/11 mastermind Khalid Sheikh Mohammed," the Associated Press reported in 2011.[23] "Pakistani authorities are clearly aware of Khalil's whereabouts," AP continued. But they leave him alone, just as they tolerate other Kashmiri militant groups nurtured by the military and its intelligence agency to use against India."

And like LeT, Pakistan has done nothing to crack down on HuM and its activities in Afghanistan and Kashmir.

Jaish-e-Mohammed

The US government has listed Jaish-e-Mohammed (JeM) as a Foreign Terrorist organization and its leader, Massod Azhar, as a specially designated global terrorist for their ties to al Qaeda and other jihadist groups.

Like LeT and HuM, JeM is supported by Pakistan's military and ISI because it is hostile to India and wages jihad in Afghanistan. In its 2010 designation of Azhar, the US Treasury Department said that "JeM recruitment posters in Pakistan

---

[20] Terror leader lives freely near Pakistani capital. (2011, June 16). *Dawn*. Retrieved from http://www.dawn.com/news/636965/terror-leader-lives-freely-near-pakistani-capital

[21] Gall, Carlotta, Zubair Shah, Pir and Schmitt, Eric. (2011, June 23). Seized Phone Offers Clues to Bin Laden's Pakistani Links. *The New York Times*. Retrieved from http://www.nytimes.com/2011/06/24/world/asia/24pakistan.html See also: Joscelyn, Thomas. (2011, June 24). Bin Laden's courier tied to Pakistani-backed terror group. The Long War Journal. Retrieved from http://www.longwarjournal.org/archives/2011/06/nyt_bin_ladens_couri.php

[22] U.S. Department of State. (2016, June 30). State Department Terrorist Designations. Retrieved from http://www.state.gov/r/pa/prs/ps/2016/06/259219.htm

[23] Terror leader lives freely near Pakistani capital. (2011, June 16). *Dawn*. Retrieved from http://www.dawn.com/news/636965/terror-leader-lives-freely-near-pakistani-capital

Bill Roggio   July 12, 2016

contained a call from Azhar for volunteers to join the fight in Afghanistan against Western forces."[24]

JeM was implicated along with the Lashkar-e-Taiba as being behind the Dec. 13, 2001 attack on the Indian Parliament building in New Delhi. Sheikh Ahmed Saeed Omar, a close associate of Azhar, was behind the kidnapping of Wall Street Journal reporter Daniel Pearl.[25] Pearl was later beheaded.

Most recently, Indian officials implicated JeM in the January 2016 assault on an Pathankot Air Force Base in India.[26] Like other attacks, Indian intelligence intercepted phone call of Pakistan-based handlers directing the assault team as they attacked the base.[27]

Despite JeM's terrorist activities, Pakistan has not taken action against the group. India has made repeated requests for extradition of Azhar, only to be ignored.[28]

A failure to act

Pakistan's intransigence towards jihadist groups has not escaped the attention of the US government. In its Country Reports on Terrorism 2015, the State Department issued a scathing rebuke of Pakistan's failure to police jihadist groups in the region.[29]

---

[24] Roggio, Bill. (2010, November 4). *The Long War Journal.* Retrieved from http://www.longwarjournal.org/archives/2010/11/us_treasury_sanction_1.php

[25] Suspected Mastermind of Pearl Kidnapping Arrested. (2002, February 12). *CNN.* Retrieved from http://transcripts.cnn.com/TRANSCRIPTS/0202/12/bn.02.html

[26] Roggio, Bill. (2016, January 2). Jaish-e-Mohammed suspected in assault on Indian airbase. *The Long War Journal.* Retrieved from http://www.longwarjournal.org/archives/2016/01/jaish-e-mohammed-suspected-in-assault-on-indian-airbase.php

[27] Tiwary, Deeptiman. (2016, January 10). Pathankot: For 20 hours, terrorists hid in elephant grass. *The Indian Express.* Retrieved from http://indianexpress.com/article/india/india-news-india/pathankot-for-20-hours-terrorists-hid-in-elephant-grass/

[28] Express News Service. (2016, April 9). India to send fresh request to UN against Masood Azhar. *The Indian Express.* Retrieved from http://indianexpress.com/article/india/india-news-india/india-to-send-fresh-request-to-un-against-masood-azhar/

[29] Country Reports on Terrorism 2015. (2016, June 2). *United States Department of State Publication.* Retrieved from http://www.longwarjournal.org/wp-content/uploads/2016/06/2016-State-Department-Country-Report-on-Terrorism.pdf

Bill Roggio   July 12, 2016

"Pakistan did not take substantial action against the Afghan Taliban or HQN, or substantially limit their ability to threaten US interests in Afghanistan," the report noted.

"Pakistan has also not taken sufficient action against other externally-focused groups such as Lashkar-e-Taiba (LeT) and Jaish-e-Mohammad (JeM), which continued to operate, train, organize, and fundraise in Pakistan," State continued. Additionally, State noted that groups continue to fundraise without consequence and Hafiz Saeed "was able to make frequent public appearances in support of the organization's objectives," without Pakistan raising a finger to stop him.[30]

State did not explain why Pakistan refuses to crack down on terrorist groups in its midst, but it is clear that the military and government considers jihadist organizations as a strategic asset and some see the jihadists as their ideological brethren.

---

[30] Roggio, Bill. (2016, June 3). 'Pakistan did not take substantial action against Afghan Taliban' or Haqqani Network: State Department. *The Long War Journal*. Retrieved from http://www.longwarjournal.org/archives/2016/06/pakistan-did-not-take-substantial-action-against-the-afghan-taliban-or-haqqani-network-state-department.php

Mr. SALMON. Thank you.
Dr. Bacon.

STATEMENT OF TRICIA BACON, PH.D., ASSISTANT
PROFESSOR, AMERICAN UNIVERSITY

Ms. BACON. Good afternoon. It is an honor to appear before you today to discuss Pakistan's policies toward militant groups. Thank you very much for this opportunity.

After the terrorist attack on Easter Sunday in Lahore that killed 70 people, Pakistani leaders reiterated their pledge to cease their dual track policy of treating some groups as having utility and going after only those that opposed the Pakistani State. However, unfortunately, the opposite has occurred. These distinctions have grown hardened, and the Pakistani State is not willing to reevaluate them.

Most importantly, the calculus of the Pakistani Army, the primary institution in Pakistan that wields power over these policies, remains unwavering. It is evident that no terrorist attack in Pakistan is large enough to cause them to reevaluate their position vis-a-vis their militant proxies. Instead, relations with the four major proxy groups—Lashkar-e-Tayyiba, Jaish-e-Mohamed, the Haqqani Network, and the Afghan Taliban—will remain a deeply entrenched component of Pakistan's national security policies.

Today I would like to outline the Pakistani security establishment's three-prong calculus vis-a-vis these organizations, in part because in order to get Pakistan to truly change its behavior, the United States will have to effect all three of these aspects of its calculus.

First and foremost, as is well-known, Pakistan's security establishment judges groups based on their utility vis-a-vis India. This is not simply about Kashmir. This is also about deep-seated fears that India is inherently aggressive toward Pakistan. This extends to Pakistan's support to the Afghan Taliban and the Haqqani Network, which stems from fears of Indian encirclement and a desire to prevent India from expanding its influence on Pakistan's western border.

As the military's efforts to achieve conventional parity with India grows increasingly futile, and the security situation in Afghanistan continues to deteriorate, Pakistan will remain committed to these policies.

Second, the security establishment evaluates militant groups based on how they affect the threat within Pakistan. Though there is extensive cross-fertilization between groups hostile to Pakistan and those seen as having utility, the so-called good militants not only largely abstain from violence within Pakistan, some also discourage other groups from engaging in violence in Pakistan. Breaking ties with the proxy groups runs the risk that they will turn their guns inward, dangerously compounding the terrorist threat within Pakistan.

Third, the Army raised its capability to dismantle and defeat militant groups. Because the civilian institutions are still not capable of truly dealing with terrorism, this task will fall to the Pakistani Army. Unfortunately, a military approach alone will be insufficient to tackle these four groups, and possibly could be counterproductive in efforts to do so.

It is worth briefly noting that relationships have evolved, especially since the 1990s when the Army provided extensive active assistance to a number of proxy organizations. This included resources, weapons, training, and even cover fire to enable cross-border infiltrations. In essence, it operated in the trenches with militant groups. U.S. and international pressure has shifted the way these relationships function.

By far, the most important asset that the Pakistani State continues to provide is safe haven and protection. The amount of active assistance has decreased. However, in this current environment, safe haven is also the most important asset that Pakistan could provide for these groups. All four organizations are highly capable and almost entirely self-sufficient other than their need for safe haven.

They have other sources of funding and weapons and equipment, as well as a sizeable cadre of capable and experienced operatives. They no longer rely on the Pakistani State for these things. The Pakistani Army did its job well. The remaining asset that they need and that they receive is safe haven. Yet the Army's relationship with Lashkar-e-Tayyiba, Jaish-e-Mohamed, the Haqqani Network, and the Afghan Taliban have proven resilient. These are the relationships that survived the tremendous fallout from 9/11 and the aftermath.

While we have been deeply dissatisfied with Pakistan's counterterrorism efforts, once-friendly militants saw Pakistan's cooperation with the United States as a betrayal, and they turned their guns against their patron. For Pakistan, it has been the worst of both worlds.

While the first rationale still dominates, all three reasons—the proxy group's utility against India and Afghanistan, their mitigation of the domestic threat and ability to worsen it, and the Pakistani State's limited ability to confront them—mutually reinforced the security establishment's ongoing relationship with militant proxies and ensure that these ties will remain intact for the foreseeable future.

I admit that I am skeptical of Pakistani pledges that they will deal with the ''good militants'' once they have taken care of the hostile ones. The bad militants, in their view, are not going away, in part because they work closely with the good militants. In the meantime, the so-called good militants will grow stronger, and the Pakistani State will be even more—will have an even more difficult task confronting them in the future.

I hope that by shedding light on the situation it will help the United States to better respond and manage the challenges ahead.

With that, I thank you for your attention and look forward to your questions.

[The prepared statement of Ms. Bacon follows:]

Dr. Tricia Bacon

Assistant Professor

American University

House Committee on Foreign Affairs

July 12, 2016

Pakistan: Friend of Foe in the Fight Against Terrorism?

Good afternoon. It is an honor to appear before you today to discuss Pakistan's connections to terrorist organizations. Thank you for this opportunity.

After the terrorist attack on Easter Sunday that killed over 70 people in Lahore, Pakistani military and civilian leaders repeated their pledge to cease the dual track policy of viewing some terrorists as having utility and seeing others as posing a threat. However, in fact, the opposite has occurred; those distinctions have hardened and grown resistant to change instead. Most importantly, the calculus of the primary institution in Pakistan that wields power over these policies remains unwavering: the Pakistani Army.

Thus, it appears that there is no terrorist attack in Pakistan large enough to persuade the security establishment to abdicate the so-called "good militants." By "good militants" I mean those groups that the Pakistani security establishment sees as having utility. Instead, its relationships with the anti-India Punjabi groups Lashkar-e-Tayyiba and Jaish-e-Mohamed as well as with the Afghan insurgent groups, the Haqqani Network and the Afghan Taliban, will remain a deeply entrenched component of Pakistan's foreign and domestic security policies. One important reason that terrorist attacks in Pakistan do not alter the Army's calculus vis-à-vis these four groups is that, for the most part, they do not engage in violence in Pakistan. They concentrate their efforts outside of Pakistan, primarily in Afghanistan and, in the case of Lashkar-e-Tayyiba and Jaish-e-Mohamed, in India as well.

This mindset reflects the Pakistani security establishment's three-pronged calculus towards militant groups, which I will focus on in my testimony today.

First and foremost, Pakistan's security establishment judges groups based on their utility vis-à-vis India based on its deep-seated belief and fear that India is inherently aggressive towards Pakistan and its ongoing dispute with India over Kashmir. Lacking the means to resolve its security competition with India, Pakistan retains relations with militant groups opposed to India and, by extension, Afghanistan as an integral part of its regional strategy. This includes Pakistan's support for the Afghan Taliban and the Haqqani Network, which stems from Pakistani fears about Indian encirclement and a desire to prevent India from expanding its influence on Pakistan's western border. The Pakistani security establishment has successfully imbued a narrative in Pakistani society that emphasizes an existential danger to Pakistan from India; privileges the military as the only reliable provider of security for Pakistan; and thereby justifies its ongoing relations with militant groups. As the military's efforts to achieve conventional parity with India grow increasingly futile and as the security situation in Afghanistan deteriorates, it will continue to see utility in its militant partners.

Second, the security establishment evaluates militant groups based how they affect the threat in Pakistan. The so-called "good militants" not only abstain from attacks in Pakistan, some, particularly Lashkar-e-Tayyiba, discourage others from engaging in violence in Pakistan as well. In addition, the security establishment surely recognizes that a break in relations with these groups would dramatically increase the terrorist threat in Pakistan beyond the Army's and the civilian government's limited capacity to manage it. Breaking ties with the proxy groups runs the risk that they will turn their guns inward, dangerously compounding the terrorist threat in Pakistan.

Third, the Army weighs its capability to dismantle and defeat militant groups. Since Pakistan still lacks the requisite civilian institutions to deal with terrorism, confronting the "good militants" would fall to the Army. Yet a military approach alone will be insufficient and perhaps even counter-productive to deal with the problem. In the case of Lashkar-e-Tayyiba and Jaish-e-Mohamed, any confrontation would occur in the Army's Punjab heartland and would likely face resistance from within the Army and from the Punjab population. Should the Army choose to confront the Haqqani Network and the Afghan Taliban, it would exacerbate the already precarious security situations in the Federally Administered Tribal Areas and Balochistan, respectively.

In assessing the Army's four main proxy groups' capability and their relationship with the Pakistani security establishment, it is worth briefly noting how relations with them have evolved. In the 1990s, the Army provided them and other groups with active assistance, which included resources, weapons, training, and even cover fire or shellings to enable cross-border infiltrations. In essence, it operated in the trenches with its proxy militant groups.

Under U.S. and international pressure, the security establishment altered the way it cooperates with its militant proxies, and its proxies have adapted as well. Currently, by far the most important asset that the security establishment provides is safe haven and protection. Overall, this is a less active form of support than in the past. Providing safe haven only involves *not* acting against groups, though the security services take it further and actively provide protection to their proxies as well. In the current environment, safe haven is also the most important asset the Army could provide for these groups. Under the protection of the Pakistani security establishment, Lashkar-e-Tayyiba, Jaish-e-Mohamed, the Afghan Taliban, and the Haqqani Network have become highly capable and almost entirely self-sufficient organizations, other than their need for haven. They have ample other sources of funding, weapons, and equipment, as well as sizeable cadres of capable and experienced operatives. The Pakistani Army did its job well, and these groups no longer rely on the Army's active support. They still sometimes benefit from more active support, such as the Inter-Services Intelligence's assistance to Lashkar-e-Tayyiba in preparing for the 2008 Mumbai attacks, but the essential remaining asset they receive from the Army is safe haven. And, it bears repeating, all four groups depend on that safe haven.

The centrality of safe haven is important to recognize because it also influences the kind of leverage that the Army has over its proxy groups. The Army could re-commence larger-scale, more active forms of support. However, for now, U.S., Indian, and international pressure have led it to dramatically reduce such support, and the leverage that the Army has over its proxy groups is mostly coercive. Its main power comes from its ability to expand and restrict their safe haven.

Yet the Army's relationships with Lashkar-e-Tayyiba, Jaish-e-Mohamed, the Haqqani Network, and the Afghan Taliban have proven resilient. These are the relationships that survived the tremendous fallout from 9/11 and its aftermath. While the United States has been deeply unsatisfied with

Pakistan's counterterrorism efforts and cooperation, once-friendly militants saw Pakistan's cooperation with the United States as a betrayal and turned their violence against their patron. For Pakistan, it was the worst of both worlds. However, these four groups retained their relationships with the Pakistani state and have benefitted enormously from it.

While the first rationale still dominates in the Pakistani security establishment's calculus, all three reasons—the proxy groups' utility against India and Afghanistan, their mitigation of the domestic threat and ability to worsen it, and the Pakistani state's limited ability to confront them—mutually reinforce the ongoing relationship with them and ensure that these ties will remain intact for the foreseeable future.

Next I would like to discuss each organization in turn and briefly describe the nature of their relationship with the security establishment. In addition, I would like to point out the complications that may follow in the highly unlikely event that Pakistan cuts ties with them.

Lashkar-e-Tayyiba

By far the closest group to the Pakistani security establishment is the anti-India, Punjab-based organization, Lashkar-e-Tayyiba, which is the only major militant group in the region that adheres to Ahl-e-Hadithism. More than any other group, Lashkar-e-Tayyiba is woven into the fabric of Pakistani society and operates as an extension of the Pakistani state. It is steadfastly loyalty to its patron, even demonstrating domestic utility by challenging the legitimacy of extremist groups that attack Pakistan. In so doing, Lashkar also parrots the Army's narrative that terrorist attacks in Pakistan are the product of a "foreign hand," an oblique reference to India, Afghanistan, and the United States. For example, earlier this year, Hafiz Saeed—the leader of Jamaat ul-Dawa (JUD), and, by extension, Lashkar-e-Tayyiba—publicly accused the United States and India of supporting the Islamic State's inroads into Pakistan.

Jamaat ul-Dawa, which engages in social service provision and proselytization efforts in Pakistan, has long attempted to falsely portray itself as separate from Lashkar. However, in an indication of how secure the organization is in Pakistan, JUD recently shed this obvious fiction of separation when it claimed a Lashkar attack in Kashmir in February on Twitter.

In another indication of Lashkar's comfortable position in Pakistan, the group recently set up so-called "sharia courts" in Punjab, essentially creating a parallel judicial system, by some accounts with support from local law enforcement. This reflects the way in which the group occupies space unfilled by the government, though with the government's support and in support of it.

If this evidence is not sufficiently persuasive to convey the depth of Lashkar's safe haven and protection in Pakistan, I would point out that Lashkar is the only currently operating terrorist group that I am aware of that has not lost its top founding leaders in nearly 30 years *or* experienced an organizational splinter of consequence.

Though Lashkar-e-Tayyiba has not conducted a major attack in India since the 2008 Mumbai attacks, the reverberations of this attack are still being felt as other groups have adopted a similar modus operandi after the "success" of the Mumbai attacks. I assess that Lashkar has not conducted another major attack primarily because of pressure from the Pakistani Army to abstain from attacks that could cause international pressure. However, this restraint has come at a cost for the United States and Afghanistan, as Lashkar has re-directed its operatives to Afghanistan in order to keep them engaged and loyal. Lashkar probably fears that if it does not provide an outlet for its fighters, they will defect to other, more active and less constrained organizations.

However, should a rupture in relations between the Army and Lashkar occur, a Lashkar unleashed from the Pakistani state would be far less restrained in its violence against India and in Afghanistan. In the highly unlikely event that the Army breaks ties with Lashkar, we can expect Lashkar to engage in large-scale attacks in India. It is also possible that Lashkar would expand its operations outside of South Asia.

Jaish-e-Mohamed

Jaish-e-Mohamed—another Punjab-based, anti-India organization—has recently re-emerged after a period of relative quiescence. After 9/11, Jaish-e-Mohamed grew deeply divided about whether to retain a relationship with the Pakistani state. This resulted in an organizational split with a faction of the group turning against the Pakistani state and becoming involved in numerous attacks in Pakistan.

This split badly damaged the pro-state faction of Jaish-e-Mohamed, but the group appears to have recovered, mostly notably conducting an attack in January against an Indian Air Force station. Many observers suspect that Jaish's recovery was due in significant part to support from the security establishment, specifically as part of its efforts to coopt hostile elements. Jaish provides an avenue for militants who turned against the state to return to the pro-state fold. In order to make Jaish an appealing group to return to, the security establishment is apparently willing to allow it some latitude to strike in India. Jaish-e-Mohamed is intimately familiar with the faux crackdown charade enacted by security services that followed its attack in January and will, yet again, wait until international pressure subsides to re-emerge unscathed.

Unlike the other proxy groups, Jaish-e-Mohamed members have engaged in some sectarian violence in Pakistan and probably continue to do so. The group adheres to Deobandism, and is integrated into the broader Deobandi militant tapestry, which includes numerous anti-state elements and has been responsible for much of the sectarian violence in Pakistan.

If the Army were to turn against Jaish-e-Mohamed, it would likely cause extensive violence in Punjab, which is Pakistan's most populous and politically powerful province, and home to the Prime Minister. Both Jaish-e-Mohamed and Lashkar-e-Tayyiba are deeply embedded in the fabric of Punjabi society. Consequently, a confrontation in Punjab could even threaten to the stability of Pakistan.

The Haqqani Network & The Afghan Taliban

As mentioned earlier, the Haqqani Network and the Afghan Taliban also enjoy sanctuary in Pakistan. Both have personnel operating in major cities in Pakistan, but concentrate their presence in areas of Pakistan directly across the border from their respective strongholds in Afghanistan. Specifically, the Afghan Taliban has an extensive presence in Balochistan, and the Haqqanis find haven in the Federally Administered Tribal Areas.

Of the two, the security establishment is believed to enjoy closer relations with the Haqqanis. Their relationship pre-dates the formation of the Afghan Taliban. Notably, the Haqqanis have been willing to strike Indian targets in Afghanistan, almost certainly at the Pakistani military's behest. The Haqqani Network's extensive infrastructure in North Waziristan was one of the main reasons that the Pakistani Army was so reluctant to conduct military operations there. When the Army finally launched Operation Zarb-e-Azb in 2014, the Haqqani Network had suspiciously relocated to Kurram, strongly suggesting that the group was forewarned of the impending operation. Though the Haqqanis emerged unscathed, some reports indicate that the military operations in North Waziristan caused tensions between the Haqqani Network and the Pakistani security services. However, with the Haqqani Network's leader, Siraj Haqqani, occupying the number two position in the Afghan Taliban, this relationship is as important as ever to the Army. While there is no affection on either side, both the Pakistani security establishment and the Haqqanis recognize that they need one another in equal measure. In contrast to the relationships with the Punjab-based groups, Pakistan's relationships with the Afghan Taliban and Haqqani Network are based on convenience and mutual interests and managed through coercion.

Unfortunately, Pakistan believes it cannot simultaneously uproot the Afghan militant groups from their haven in Pakistan and deliver them to the negotiating table. In the unlikely event that Pakistan moves against the Afghan insurgent groups' safe havens, it would lose its leverage to pressure them to engage in peace talks. From Pakistan's perspective, its investment in supporting the Afghan Taliban and the Haqqani Network has paid dividends by ensuring that it has a place at the negotiating table and will have a say in Afghanistan's future. Put simply, it is not going to throw away that investment now.

In pointing out the consequences of unlikely ruptures in Pakistan's relations with these four groups, I by no means am justifying or excusing them. Instead, I wish to point out the Frankenstein situation that Pakistan has created for itself and that any future efforts to extricate itself from it will come at a cost and produce new threats with which the United States would have to grapple.

Dealing with the "Bad Militants"

We've talked about the so called "good militants," but now I would like to conclude my testimony by discussing the Pakistani security establishment's approach to hostile militants. As is well known, Pakistan's counterterrorism cooperation with the United States has been critical to the progress made against al-Qaida. In its efforts against hostile militants, Pakistan has sustained tremendous losses and expended significant resources. It has engaged in—or at least acquiesced to—cooperation with the United States that was unpopular domestically and that stoked hostile militants' antipathy.

Of note, fatalities to date this year in Pakistan from terrorist attacks are substantially lower than in recent years, notwithstanding the attack in Lahore on Easter that killed over 70 people. Some of this decrease in violence is attributable to the military operations in FATA, which pushed many Pakistani Taliban members and other hostile militants across the border into Afghanistan.

Nonetheless, Pakistan faces a resilient threat from the likes of the Pakistani Taliban, Lashkar-e-Jhangvi, al-Qaida, and others. Its effectiveness in dealing with these threats has been and will continue to be seriously hampered by its false dichotomization of "good militants" and "bad militants"; its vacillation between appeasement and scorched earth tactics; and its self-serving and erroneous focus on external actors as the source of its internal threat.

First, and most important, Pakistan's counter-terrorism efforts will remain hamstrung by the artificial boundary it has attempted to erect between good militants and bad militants. The categorization of militants as friendly or hostile fails to account for the inter-twined nature of the

Deobandi militant groups in the region. For the Deobandi militant groups, organizational loyalties and membership are fluid and inter-organizational cooperation is common. This means that Deobandi militant groups allied with the Pakistani state, specifically Jaish-e-Mohamed, the Afghan Taliban, and the Haqqani Network, collaborate extensively with groups hostile to the Pakistani state, including the Pakistani Taliban and Lashkar-e-Jhangvi. In addition, al-Qaida, though not Deobandi, is fully integrated into this militant network and works closely with these groups as well. Groups hostile to Pakistan have exploited this loophole, such as to find safe haven in North Waziristan under the Haqqani Network's protection until military operations finally commenced in 2014.

Second, Pakistan's long-term success against militants will suffer from its proclivity towards cooptation and appeasement. It has repeatedly come to modus vivendis with militant groups that are willing to concentrate their violence outside of Pakistan, usually in Afghanistan. These arrangements are often unstable and provide groups with breathing room to recover and regroup before returning to violence in Pakistan. In the meantime, Afghan and Coalition Forces and Afghan civilians bear the brunt of these arrangements. It is not a sustainable solution, and it comes at the expense of Afghanistan's security.

Third, on the other end of the spectrum, the security establishment uses scorched earth tactics to eliminate militants, which includes "forced disappearances" and "encounters," i.e. extra-judicial detentions and killings. With a civilian judicial system unable to effectively prosecute terrorists, the military's tactics were given the veneer of legality when the civilian government acquiesced to allow military courts to deal with terrorist suspects and re-instated the death penalty in January 2015.

While few may lament the removal of hardened terrorists with significant blood on their hands, the security services' impunity causes two major issues. First, it encourages a cycle of revenge and retaliation with militants that has no end. The cycle of violence will continue in perpetuity as long as death is the primary way of dealing with militants that cannot be coopted. Put bluntly: the scope of the terrorist threat in Pakistan is not one that Pakistan can kill its way out of.

In addition, this impunity threatens Pakistan's civil society, the media, and the prospects for democracy in Pakistan. These same tactics are used against vocal critics of the military and dissidents in Balochistan. The authority to kill and to disappear people is not limited to irreconcilable terrorists; it extends to others deemed adversaries of the military's position of power in Pakistan.

Yet with less than six months left before the 21st Amendment expires, there is little sign that the civilian criminal justice system has undergone the necessary reforms to enable it to effectively handle terrorism-related cases. The civilians have, once again, failed to take the steps needed to play a meaningful and constructive role in combating extremism.

Lastly, the Pakistani Army's diagnosis of the sources of the domestic terrorist threat virtually guarantees that it will not apply an effective long-term solution. The Army persists in seeing the domestic threat as driven not by blowback from its decades of support for militant groups, but by a "foreign hand," a veiled reference to India, Afghanistan, or the United States. By looking outward for the source of the threat, the Army thereby absolves itself of its role in nurturing extremist groups and religious intolerance for decades and ignores the domestic drivers of extremism. As a result, it is unlikely that the Army will make the requisite changes to truly degrade the threat, rather than temporarily disrupting it.

Conclusion

I realize that the prognosis that I have offered is grim. It includes a Pakistan committed to relations with highly capable and dangerous militant groups. The relationships between the Pakistani security establishment and Lashkar-e-Tayyiba, Jaish-e-Mohamed, the Haqqani Network, and the Afghan Taliban may bend, but they are unlikely to break. I see the decrease in violence from terrorist attacks as temporary in light of Pakistan's inaccurate diagnosis of the source of the threat as externally driven, its support for groups that work closely with its adversaries, deep systematic flaws in Pakistan's counter-extremism institutions, and the ongoing cycle of retribution, not to mention the persistent underlying conditions fueling radicalization. I am skeptical of Pakistani pledges that they will deal with the "good militants" once they have taken care of the "bad militants." The bad militant problems are not going away and, in the meantime, the "good militants" will grow stronger and will become even more difficult for the Pakistani security establishment to confront. I hope that by shedding light on this situation, it will help the United States to better respond and manage the challenges ahead.

With that, I thank you for your attention and look forward to your questions.

Mr. SALMON. Thank you very much.

This has been very, very enlightening. You know, when I have done town hall meetings back in my district, this probably gets more people's dander up than anything else. And I know when we have had votes on the floor to either defund or significantly reduce the funding to Pakistan, it has always done very well.

Most of the voters that I come into contact with wonder why in the heck we give people money that actually aid and abet those that commit terrorist acts across the globe. The other thing that I have got to wonder, the other countries that we try to influence, don't they think we are a bunch of chumps? I mean, that is the other thing that I have got to wonder is, you know, they see us as being so stupid.

And it kind of reminds me—you know, I wasn't there, but in some of the movies I have seen about how the old Mafia used to deal with businesses, come take money from them to protect them, so to speak, it kind of seems reminiscent of that to me. It is like paying the Mafia off, but no good is going to come of it in the end.

So, Mr. Roggio, you suggested that we just cut off all funding completely to Pakistan and go ahead and move with whatever is required to declare them a State Sponsor of Terrorism, and then also, you know, look at limiting travel for those from Pakistan or the United States and possibly even look at trade.

I am a believer that if we just cut off the funding, it is not going to be enough. If we just cut off the funding, I don't think it is going to be significant enough to them, to the other resources they get from the bad guys, and so I am wondering, why in the world have we continued to pursue this policy of, you know, I don't know, giving them money when we know all the bad things that they are doing. Why have we done this policy in the first place?

I guess I could understand in the first place why we did it, because there was some assistance in the war with terrorism with Afghanistan. But now I don't understand the rationale. Could you or Ambassador—any of you—give me the rationale, why we are still doing it, do you—and what other options do we have right now?

Ambassador KHALILZAD. Well, I believe that part of the reason for continuing to pursue this approach has been the belief—and Pakistanis are very clever in manipulating us, I have to say that, number one—the belief that they are about to change. You cannot believe, Chairman, that so many times that they notice that things are moving possibly toward a change in our policy, then at that time they take an initiative to make it hard for us to then actually go through with it. So they know how to——

Mr. SALMON. Work us.

Ambassador KHALILZAD. Right. And you have noticed recently when there has been, again, pressure on them to—isolating them, they reach out to distinguished Members of Congress, and they invite them for visits, they charm them, they promise, once again, and even exact statement from ourselves that are surprising in the face of facts as they are because we are a polite people and we don't want to insult our hosts.

So I think the Pakistani ability to manipulate by their actions in part has been a factor, but——

Mr. SALMON. We have been manipulated by a lot of countries. North Korea is an example. And, I mean, I will go back to there is a word for that. They are making chumps out of us.

Ambassador KHALILZAD. Well, they are playing—if I might use an undiplomatic term, but we have been patsies.

Mr. SALMON. Patsy, chump.

Ambassador KHALILZAD. Yeah, right.

Mr. SALMON. Idiot.

Ambassador KHALILZAD. Well——

Mr. SALMON. Well, most Americans out there see through all of this, and yet, you know, our so-called leaders don't really get it. I can't even contemplate why on God's green earth we even thought for a nanosecond about the F-16 sale. I am glad that it has been scuttled, but none of it makes any sense at all.

Mr. Roggio, you had a comment.

Mr. ROGGIO. Yes, just quickly. I mean, I think with the F-16 sales, I mean, obviously, someone is going to make money off of that, and there is a lobby in Congress, of course, to push sales through like that. No secret.

But I also think that a lot of people in the case of the aid that is going to Pakistan do think that it is going to do good. But the reality is is the Pakistani madrassas are still cranking out thousands upon thousands of potential jihadists, who are going to join the Taliban or any of these other so-called good militant groups, good Taliban groups.

So whatever we are providing, it is not working. It is not changing Pakistani society. It is not changing Pakistani education. So I think there certainly is—I understand that we think we are doing good, but in the end, as you said, they are treating us like chumps. They recognize it, and we are more than willing to keep handing out money to Pakistan, so why wouldn't they take it?

Mr. SALMON. I just have one other quick question, because we have all asked questions from the State Department when they have come about Dr. Afridi and what they have done to try to secure his release. And every time it is the same, you know, mantra, ''Oh, we talked to them about that.'' Are they doing enough?

Mr. ROGGIO. Absolutely not. Look, he is being held in order to punish the United States for what we did to kill Osama bin Laden. By all rights, he should be a hero in Pakistan, as he is here, and he is being held to punish us, to punish him, and to send a message to any other Pakistani willing to help us that, if you go ahead and do this, this is your fate. Honestly, I am surprised he is alive.

Mr. SALMON. Thank you.

Mr. Sherman.

Mr. SHERMAN. I will pick up right there. Ambassador, what if we cut half of all aid to Pakistan until Dr. Afridi and his family is here in the United States, what would be the reaction of the Pakistani Government? And do you expect the Pakistani people are going to riot in favor of imprisoning Dr. Afridi?

Ambassador KHALILZAD. Well, I think that making a lot of aid, you said half, conditional I think will have more of an impact. I don't anticipate——

Mr. SHERMAN. Well, obviously, it has more of an impact on the feckless policy we have had so far, but——

Ambassador KHALILZAD. Right.

Mr. SHERMAN [continuing]. What will be the reaction in Pakistan to that? Are they—first of all, at minimum, maybe they take us up on it, we save almost $1 billion. That would be a good thing to a lot of——

Ambassador KHALILZAD. Even if they don't take us up, we would have saved some money.

Mr. SHERMAN. Right. That is the point I am making.

Ambassador KHALILZAD. Right. But I think that my experience in dealing with Pakistan is that they would only give you something when they know that you are——

Mr. SHERMAN. Okay. Their counterargument on all this is they can't give us Dr. Afridi, because, oh my God, it will be some terrible circumstance in their country. If the Pakistani Government were to put Dr. Afridi and his family on a plane for the United States today, what harm would that Pakistani leader have tomorrow?

Ambassador KHALILZAD. No harm whatsoever, in my judgment, because some of these groups that rise on the street, all the groups that—based on long experience I can tell you that——

Mr. SHERMAN. They were told to riot, yes.

Ambassador KHALILZAD [continuing]. When they raised these——

Mr. SHERMAN. I want to go on to Mr. Roggio. The F–16s, they are going to be back, they are going to be asking for them. The argument is that these are the planes best suited to going after the terrorists in the frontier territories. Is there a weapon system that is less expensive, just as good as being a platform to survey, and to lob a missile at terrorists, and that poses less of a—and would not be useful in going after India? Something a lot less sophisticated.

Mr. ROGGIO. Yes, absolutely. As a matter of fact, I would say F–16s or high advanced fighter planes are overkill in conducting counterinsurgency operations, low-tech planes that could loiter over the battlefield and deliver munitions.

Mr. SHERMAN. So if they are trying to get a plane to go over the Haqqani Network, the F–16 is not the right choice.

Mr. ROGGIO. It is not the right choice. We use aircraft like this in Iraq and Afghanistan because it is what we have and what we know. But there is certainly a lot better options available.

Ambassador KHALILZAD. Sorry. If I might add, if they would arrest first Jalaluddin Haqqani, that would be an indication that they are serious about going after the Haqqani Network.

Mr. SHERMAN. Well——

Ambassador KHALILZAD. They move them around themselves to meetings and provide them with first-class housing. Made it a little hard to believe that they are going to move militarily against the Haqqani Network.

Mr. SHERMAN. Let me ask Dr. Bacon. Okay. Even a second year law student has read 1,000 cases, could recognize when the judge is citing a precedent correctly or incorrectly. Let's say there is a fatwa that comes out relevant to your work at the State Department. Do you have a State Department office that can evaluate whether that fatwa was based on a strong hadith or a weak hadith? Who do you go to? Who knows?

Ms. BACON. When I was at the State Department—I left in 2013—there were a number of experts on political Islam.

Mr. SHERMAN. Political Islam. But were these people who had read 1,000 fatwas and who knew the difference between a strong and a weak hadith? Or were these Princeton graduates who had studied the history of the Ottoman Empire?

Ms. BACON. There were both. And within the intelligence community, there certainly are a number of people who are experts on it.

Mr. SHERMAN. Well, let's go like to State Department. Is there a single person whose job description says they have got to be as knowledgeable about Islamic law and Islamic jurisprudence and Islamic theology as a graduate of the chief school, institute in Cairo, for example?

Ms. BACON. Especially when it comes to the countering violent extremism efforts, there has been a number of people who have been brought on to focus on——

Mr. SHERMAN. Can you name somebody who would know——

Ms. BACON. I am no longer at the State Department, so I would defer to——

Mr. SHERMAN. Okay. Who was there 2 years ago, 3 years ago?

Ms. BACON. There were several people in the Bureau of Intelligence and Research who were brought on for their expertise in Islam, but I don't know who is currently there.

Mr. SHERMAN. Their expertise in Islam. So they have read English books on the history of the Ottoman Empire.

Ambassador, is there anybody who is employed by the State Department who could pass the final exams at—I forget the name. I will——

Ambassador KHALILZAD. Al-Azhar.

Mr. SHERMAN. Yes. Do we have—I know we have got a bunch that can pass the final exams at the highest levels at Princeton. Do we have a single person there that could pass medium to low grades, the institute I just——

Ambassador KHALILZAD. I have been out of the State Department now for 7 years, ago——

Mr. SHERMAN. Okay. Seven years ago, did we have anybody?

Ambassador KHALILZAD. I don't remember that—that we did.

Mr. SHERMAN. Okay. Dr. Bacon, if you could provide for the record that there is somebody at the State Department who isn't just an Ottoman history buff, but who has read thousands of fatwa, who was hired because they know the difference between a strong hadith and a weak hadith, either today or in 2013, that would be helpful.

Thank you.

Mr. SALMON. Thank you.

Mr. Rohrabacher. And before I get to Mr. Rohrabacher, we have just been pinged for a vote on the floor. And we have 10 votes, and I don't think we will be coming back afterwards. So if I could maybe get both you and Mr. Keating in.

Mr. ROHRABACHER. I will try.

Mr. SALMON. Try. Thanks.

Mr. ROHRABACHER. All right. I will go quick. I will say for the record that the Pakistani Government, the ISI, created the

Taliban, along with the Saudis, after we left when the Soviets withdrew from Afghanistan. Since that—at that time, the Pakistani Government was deeply involved with creating that regime that ended up offering safe haven to Osama bin Laden, and the murder of 3,000 Americans.

Let us note, when we went to drive out the Taliban that the Northern Alliance, with our help and our support, drove the Taliban out. Where did they drive them to? Pakistan. Where did Osama bin Laden go? Osama bin Laden, the murder of 3,000 Americans, was given safe haven for almost a decade in Pakistan. I don't know anyone who believes that the leadership of Pakistan did not know Osama bin Laden was there, right there in their country, in an urban area.

Let us note that when our troops—when our brave special forces went to bring justice to Osama bin Laden, that they had to fly very specialized helicopters, so that they wouldn't be shot down. By whom? By Pakistan. With airplanes that we had given them. This is insane.

Let us note that Pakistan still holds Dr. Afridi, the man who made it possible for us to identify Osama bin Laden, the murderer of 3,000 Americans, and they hold him in a dungeon today, which is nothing more than rubbing our face in the fact that they can do that and how much they really hate us. This is ridiculous that we give any aid whatsoever to a power like that.

For the record, the people of Balochistan are being slaughtered by this corrupt, oppressive regime. The people of Balochistan have to understand—should understand the United States is on their side because they are struggling for independence and self-determination from a corrupt, vicious, terrorist-supporting regime.

Same with the Sindhis. Same with other groups in Afghanistan. So we have a regime that murders and represses and is corrupt with their own people, and yet we still continue to give them some type of support. It is absolutely absurd.

And, Ambassador Khalilzad, we have worked together many years, I am going to ask you a tough question. When the Taliban were driven out of Afghanistan and our friends in the Northern Alliance came in and took Kabul, there was a decision made in Bonn—and I think we were both at Bonn, Germany.

The decision was, who was then going to be the leader of the new Afghanistan? Or at least in transition. I, of course, was pushing for King Zahir Shah, as were a group of us who had supported the Northern Alliance. It is my memory that you and the administration were supporting Karzai. Was that due to undue influence by the Pakistani Government on that administration, the Bush administration, as they have had undue influence on all of these administrations?

Ambassador KHALILZAD. Thank you for the statement with which I associate myself. Eloquently stated, Congressman. On this question of Karzai's choice, why Karzai was selected, the name of Karzai was first brought up by Abdullah Abdullah who was a key figure in the Northern Alliance at that time.

Mr. ROHRABACHER. Right.

Ambassador KHALILZAD. He argued that for the next phase of Afghanistan, Afghanistan needed a Pashtun leader that the Northern

Alliance could work with, and he thought that Karzai was such a Pashtun. And this was the first time that we had heard of Karzai for such a role. And Jim Dobbins, my colleague who represented us at that time—and I was in the White House then—reported that.

So, but then when we checked with others in the region and beyond, Pakistan did not object to President Karzai's choice, as well as quite a number of others.

Mr. ROHRABACHER. Let me note for the record that that was a pivotal decision that has led to problems. The problems that we are discussing today, the King of Afghanistan would have been much more independent, he was beloved by his people, he was a Pashtun, and we turned him down. And I honestly believe, like you said, we asked Pakistan for their opinions on it. Pakistan, of course, pushed for someone they could control, someone who would be consistent with their corrupt, repressive regime, and that was Karzai.

Unfortunately, now we face this challenge today. Thank you for your service. Thank all of you for your opinions.

Mr. SALMON. Thank you.

Mr. Keating. And we have 4 minutes now before the votes. Sorry.

Mr. KEATING. Thank you, Mr. Chairman. Because of the time, I am going to just ask one question I think. And it is one that confuses the public to an extent, so it is confusion or it is downright obfuscation on the part of Pakistan.

What is the role of the ISI? You know, the assassinated former Prime Minister Bhutto called the ISI a state within a state. So if you could, just in that timeframe that we have left, quickly comment on what you think that is. Are they a rogue element there that is not answerable to Prime Minister Sharif? How far does it go, in your opinion? You will have to be brief. I apologize.

Ms. BACON. I will be very brief. It is by no means a rogue institution within Pakistan, and it is not operating independently or on its own. It is an instrument and an arm of the Pakistani Army, and it is implementing the policies of the Pakistani Army. So it is not just a few officers, and it is not making policy up. It is implementing on behalf of the Pakistani Army.

Mr. ROGGIO. Yes. I concur. It is an arm of the Pakistani military. It is executing the will of the Pakistani military, which is indeed the Pakistani State. The government is really just the face of the Pakistani military.

Ambassador KHALILZAD. I concur with my colleagues.

Mr. KEATING. That is great. We can all make our rollcall. Thank you very much for your very clear and frank testimony, and I yield back.

Mr. SALMON. I thank the panel. We could go on several hours. You are amazing, and I really appreciate it.

For the record, I personally believe that we should completely cut off all funding to Pakistan. I think that would be the right first step, and give that a chance to work. And then, if we don't see any changes, we move to some of the other suggestions, Mr. Roggio, a State Sponsor of Terrorism declaration, possible economic sanctions.

And I personally believe that right now we have the worst policy that we could possibly have, and all we are doing is rewarding thugs.

So I thank the panel very, very much. I thank the gentleman. And this committee is now adjourned.

[Whereupon, at 3:01 p.m., the subcommittees were adjourned.]

A P P E N D I X

MATERIAL SUBMITTED FOR THE RECORD

JOINT SUBCOMMITTEE HEARING NOTICE
COMMITTEE ON FOREIGN AFFAIRS
U.S. HOUSE OF REPRESENTATIVES
WASHINGTON, DC 20515-6128

Subcommittee on Terrorism, Nonproliferation, and Trade
Ted Poe (R-TX), Chairman

Subcommittee on Asia and the Pacific
Matt Salmon (R-AZ), Chairman

TO: MEMBERS OF THE COMMITTEE ON FOREIGN AFFAIRS

You are respectfully requested to attend an OPEN hearing of the Committee on Foreign Affairs, to be held jointly by the Subcommittee on Terrorism, Nonproliferation, and Trade and the Subcommittee on Asia and the Pacific in Room 2172 of the Rayburn House Office Building (and available live on the Committee website at http://www.ForeignAffairs.house.gov):

DATE: Tuesday, July 12, 2016

TIME: 2:00 p.m.

SUBJECT: Pakistan: Friend or Foe in the Fight Against Terrorism?

WITNESSES: The Honorable Zalmay Khalilzad
                   Counselor
                   Center for Strategic and International Studies

                   Mr. Bill Roggio
                   Senior Editor
                   Long War Journal
                   Foundation for Defense of Democracies

                   Tricia Bacon, Ph.D.
                   Assistant Professor
                   American University

By Direction of the Chairman

The Committee on Foreign Affairs seeks to make its facilities accessible to persons with disabilities. If you are in need of special accommodations, please call 202/225-5021 at least four business days in advance of the event, whenever practicable. Questions with regard to special accommodations in general (including availability of Committee materials in alternative formats and assistive listening devices) may be directed to the Committee.

COMMITTEE ON FOREIGN AFFAIRS

MINUTES OF SUBCOMMITTEE ON ___*Terrorism, Nonproliferation, & Trade and Asia & the Pacific*___ HEARING

Day___*Tuesday*___Date___*July 12, 2016*___Room_____*2171*_____

Starting Time ___*2:02 p.m.*___ Ending Time ___*3:01 p.m.*___

Recesses |___| (___to___) (___to___) (___to___) (___to___) (___to___) (___to___)

Presiding Member(s)

Chairman Matt Salmon

Check all of the following that apply:

Open Session ☑
Executive (closed) Session ☐
Televised ☑

Electronically Recorded (taped) ☑
Stenographic Record ☑

TITLE OF HEARING:

"Pakistan: Friend or Foe in the Fight Against Terrorism?"

SUBCOMMITTEE MEMBERS PRESENT:

Reps. Salmon, Rohrabacher, Chabot, Wilson, DesJarlais, Ribble, Zeldin, Keating, Sherman, Bera, Lowenthal, Gabbard, Castro

---

NON-SUBCOMMITTEE MEMBERS PRESENT: *(Mark with an * if they are not members of full committee.)*

HEARING WITNESSES: Same as meeting notice attached? Yes ☑ No ☐
(If "no", please list below and include title, agency, department, or organization.)

STATEMENTS FOR THE RECORD: *(List any statements submitted for the record.)*

SFR submitted by Chairman Ted Poe
QFR submitted by Rep. Brad Sherman

TIME SCHEDULED TO RECONVENE _____
or
TIME ADJOURNED ___*3:01 p.m.*___

Subcommittee Staff Director

Statement for the Record

By Chairman Ted Poe

House Foreign Affairs Committee

"Pakistan: Friend or Foe in the Fight Against Terrorism?"

July 12, 2016

On May 21, 2016, a U.S. drone strike killed the leader of the Afghan Taliban, Mullah Mansour. To no one's surprise, at the time of his death Mansour was in southwestern Pakistan. The drone strike Pakistan's longstanding support for terrorist groups. For example, Pakistan openly supported the Afghan Taliban both before and after the extremists took control of Kabul in 1996.

Islamabad's connection to terrorist groups is so close that in 2011 Admiral Mike Mullen, then chairman of the U.S. Joint Chiefs of Staff testified before the Senate that "the Haqqani network acts as a veritable arm of Pakistan's Inter-Services Intelligence agency." The Inter-Services Intelligence Agency or the "ISI" is Pakistan's version of the CIA. The Haqqani Network is not a nice group of people. They have killed more Americans in the region than any other terrorist group.

A leaked NATO report in 2012 detailed Pakistan's ongoing relationship with the Taliban. The report described Pakistan's "manipulation of the Taliban senior leadership" and claimed that the government was aware of locations of senior Taliban leaders, including some who lived in the vicinity of the ISI headquarters in Islamabad.

The laundry list of evidence of Pakistan's support for terrorists goes on and on. We all remember where al-Qaeda's leader and America's most wanted terrorist Osama bin Laden was found: in Pakistan, of course. In response to the bin Laden raid, Pakistan put the doctor who helped us in jail and closed the U.S. military's supply route from Karachi port to Afghanistan for 7 months.

While Pakistan has been harboring and supporting terrorists with American blood on their hands, it also has been receiving billions in U.S. foreign assistance. In fact, Pakistan is one of the leading recipients of U.S. aid in the last 14 years. Congress has appropriated more than $33 billion to Pakistan since fiscal year 2002.

One of the ways we have given Pakistan money over the years is by reimbursing them for efforts they take to fight terrorists. But a GAO study from 2008 found that the Department of Defense could not verify the validity of Pakistan's claims. The GAO study concluded that some reimbursed costs were potentially duplicative or not based on actual activity. In 2010, Special Representative for Afghanistan and Pakistan Ambassador Richard Holbrook said that roughly 40% of Pakistan's reimbursement requests were rejected.

Each year we say that Pakistan is at the crossroads and needs to decide whether it is going to fight terrorists or fight on our side. In fact, just two months ago the State Department's Ambassador Richard Olson, used this very line. But the United States has been using this line for the last 15 years. Enough is enough.

Pakistan is playing us. They are trying to have it both ways. They want our money and they keep supporting terrorists who target Americans.

I invited Ambassador Olson to come testify before us and explain himself, but he refused. Instead, the State Department said this was a "particularly sensitive time in our relationship with Pakistan". In other words, he was afraid Pakistan would come away looking bad. Well that might be just because Pakistan is bad.

Now we have put conditions on aid to Pakistan before, requiring them to really go after terrorists if they want our money. But those conditions have always had a waiver attached to them and every year, the President has exercised that waiver. In other words, we paid Pakistan even though it did not go after terrorist groups. Well, for the first time last year, we did not include a waiver on $300 million of money for Pakistan. And guess what? Pakistan did not get the money because it had not gone after the terrorist groups. Even when there are hundreds of millions of dollars on the line, Pakistan refuses to go after terrorist groups.

The reality is that Pakistan has chosen sides. And it isn't ours. It is time to change our policy towards Pakistan. We do not need to pay Pakistan to betray us. They will do it for free.

And that's just the way it is.

Questions for the Record Submitted to

Dr. Tricia Bacon by

Representative Brad Sherman

House Foreign Affairs Committee

"Pakistan: Friend or Foe in the Fight Against Terrorism?"

July 12, 2016

Question:

Let's say there is a fatwa that comes out. Is there an office in the State Department that can evaluate whether a fatwa is based on a strong hadith or a weak hadith? Were these people who had read 1000 fatwas? Is there a single person whose job description says they have got to be as knowledgeable about Islamic law and Islamic jurisprudence and Islamic theology as a graduate of the chief school in Cairo?

Answer:

I am no longer employed at the State Department so I cannot speak to the current job descriptions of its personnel or the specific missions of its offices. During my time at the State Department, I was not involved in human resources and personnel matters, so I also cannot speak to the job descriptions of State Department personnel from that period. I defer to the State Department for questions about its offices, hiring practices, and the qualifications of its personnel, such as how many fatwas an individual has read. During my time at the State Department, I was not aware of an office in the State Department that was charged with evaluating fatwas. Such an endeavor would require, at a minimum, numerous people with substantial religious authority in Sunni, Shia, and Sufi Islam; expertise and authority in the major schools of Sunni Islam; expertise and authority in the Shia branches; expertise and authority in the Sufi orders, not to mention the various sects within Sunnism, Shi'ism, and Sufism.

However, I would note that during my tenure at the State Department and in the Intelligence Community, I worked with individuals who I regarded as experts in the different schools and sects of Islam. I do not know any scholars—State Department personnel or otherwise—who would claim to be experts on Islam writ large, given the breadth and diversity of the different traditions and schools within Islam, not to mention the regional and local variation of those traditions. Instead, individuals had appropriately narrower expertise in specific schools or sects of Islam and their local practices in different parts of the world or issues such as political Islam. Examples of former State Department personnel who I regarded as possessing expertise on some aspect of Islam include: Farah Pandith, Special Representative to Muslim Communities; Dr. Will

McCants, senior advisor for countering violent extremism; Dr. Haroon Ullah, senior advisor for policy and planning; and Dr. Ahmed al-Rahim, analyst in INR, among others. Moreover, the State Department had access to numerous scholars in academia, think tanks, and the Intelligence Community through the Intelligence Community Associates program or the Office of Outreach in the Bureau of Intelligence and Research.